You can't handle the Gru!

There's a new Gru in town!

Caution: Minions at work!

Dalmatian Press

It's good to be a Minion!

*^__^*

It's so fluffy!

How many pictures of each can you find?

Margo: ☐

Edith: ☐

Agnes: ☐

Despicable Us

How many words can you make using the letters in:
DESPICABLE ME

_____   _____

_____   _____

_____   _____

_____

_____

_____

_____

_____

_____

_____

One in a Minion!

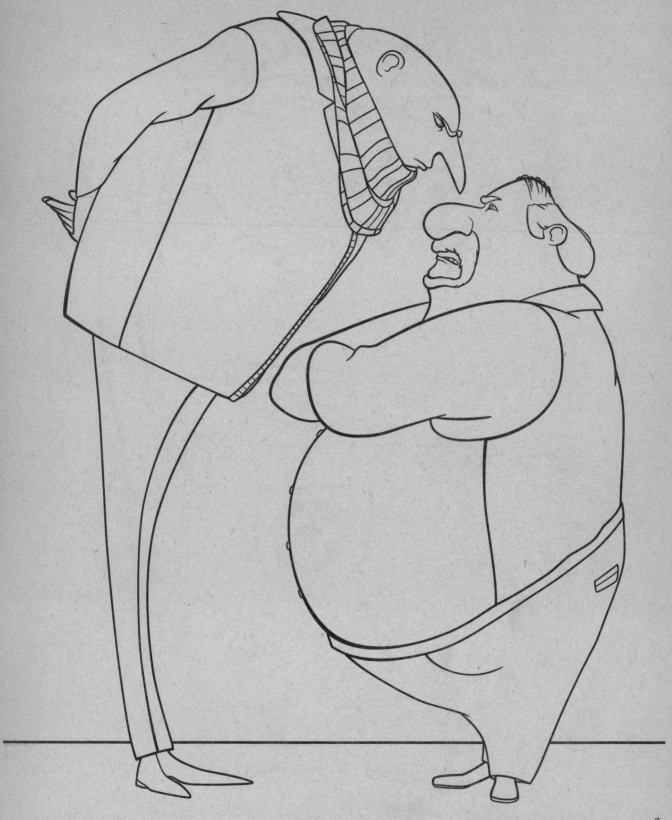

It takes a villain to catch a villain.

Team Minion

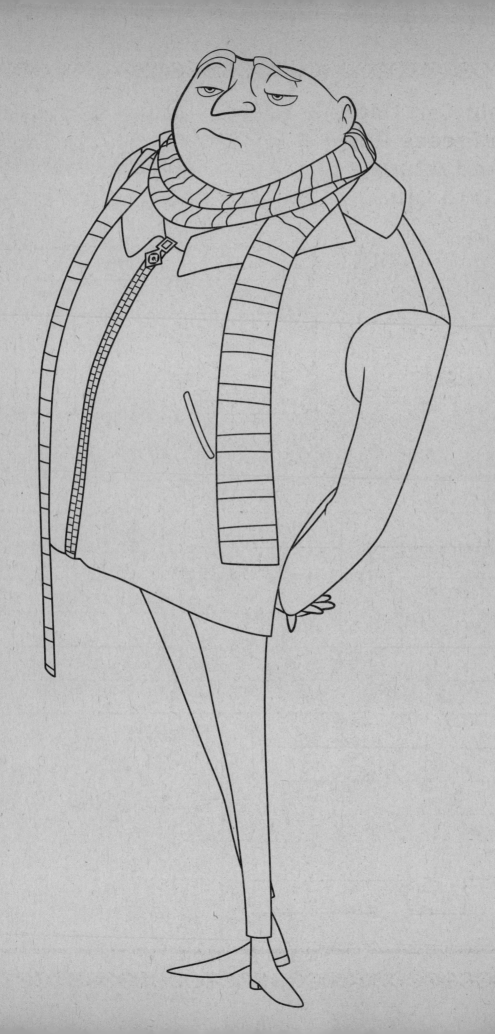

Help Carl find the Freeze Ray and return it to Gru.

START

FINISH

I'm so bad, I'm good.

Minions need love, too.

Which Agnes is different?

A

B

C

D

Your Answer: ☐

Answer: C

Connect the dots to complete the picture of the Minion.

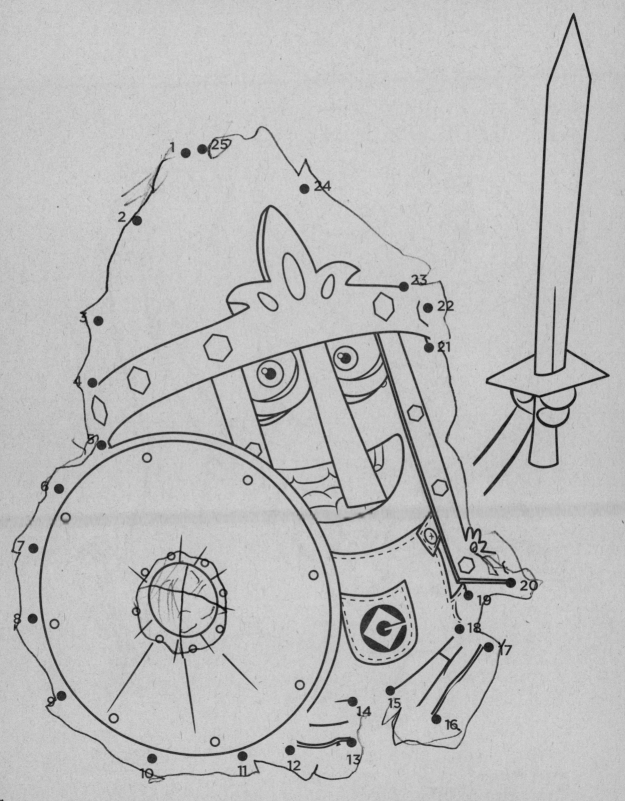

So many Minions, so little time!

One is never enough!

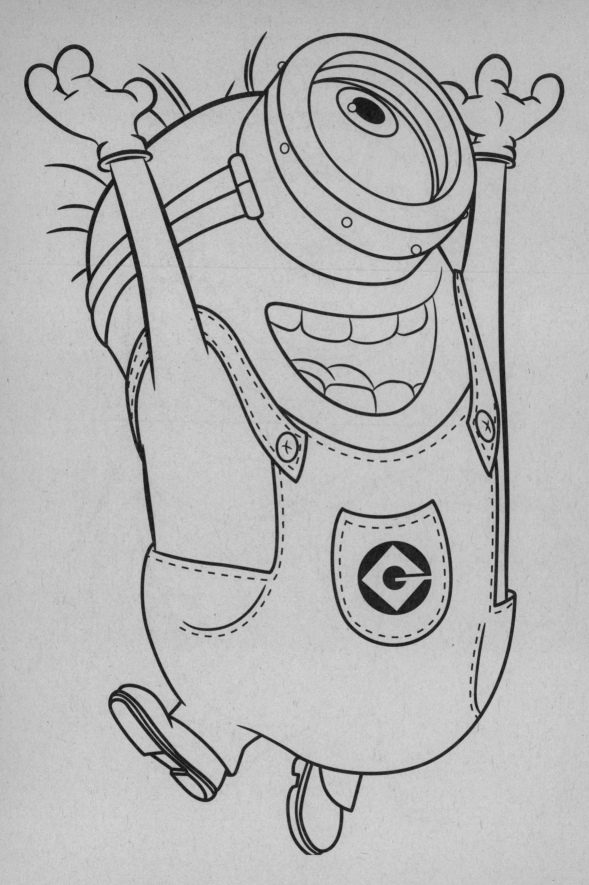

Little Minion, lots of mischief.

99% Adorable, 1% Despicable

Just a friendly Bello.

It's Doubly Despicable!

The Magnificent Minions

How many Minions do you count?

Your Answer:

Dalmatian Press

Which leads to the sundae with a cherry on top?

Answer:

Go bad or go home.

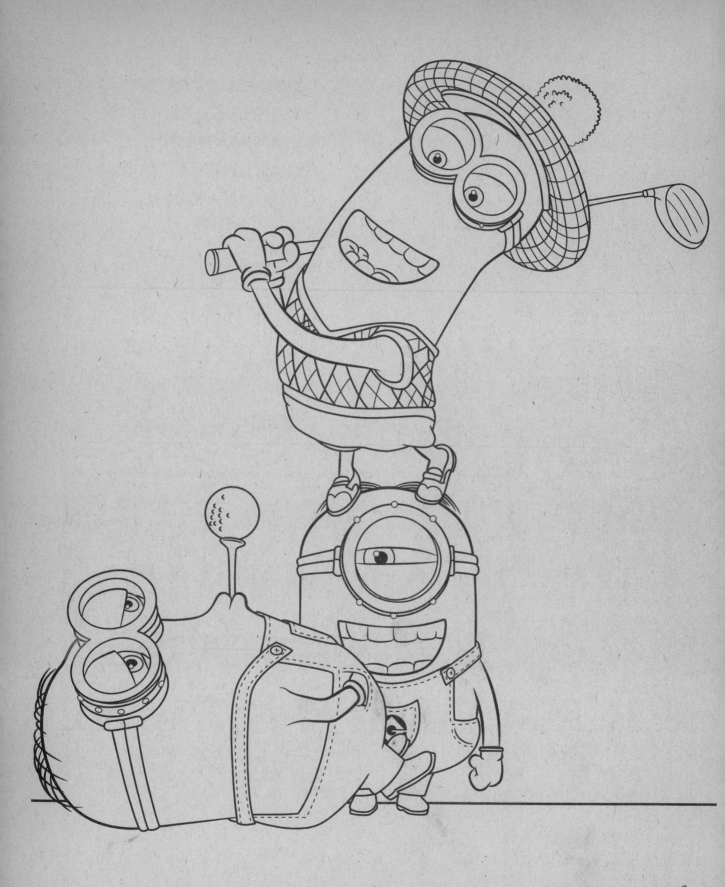

It's all fun and games until someone loses an eye.

Look up, down, across, and diagonally. Help the Minions find these despicable words!

MINION
BELLO
POOPAYE
KARATE
BANANA

```
M P J I N G T H E T N
L O Q K A R U P S N O
U O C B A N A N A Q I
K P A E D R O G T I N
J A T L O T A O C G I
Z Y N L K R L T K J M
H E T O C B D U E G P
```

Minions rock!

Quiet please – test in progress.

Why is Gru recruited by the Anti-Villain League?
Use the code to find out.

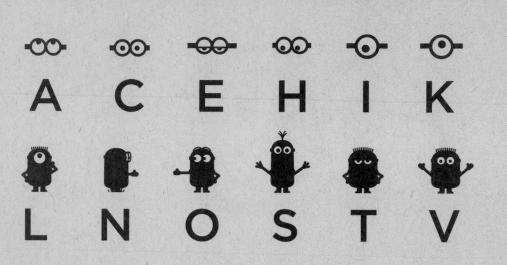

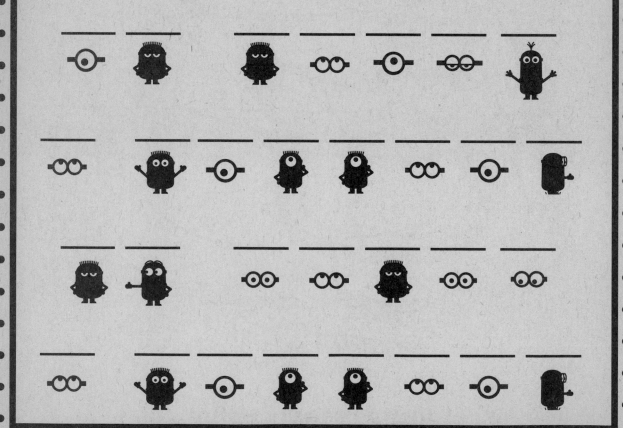

Just a friendly Bello!

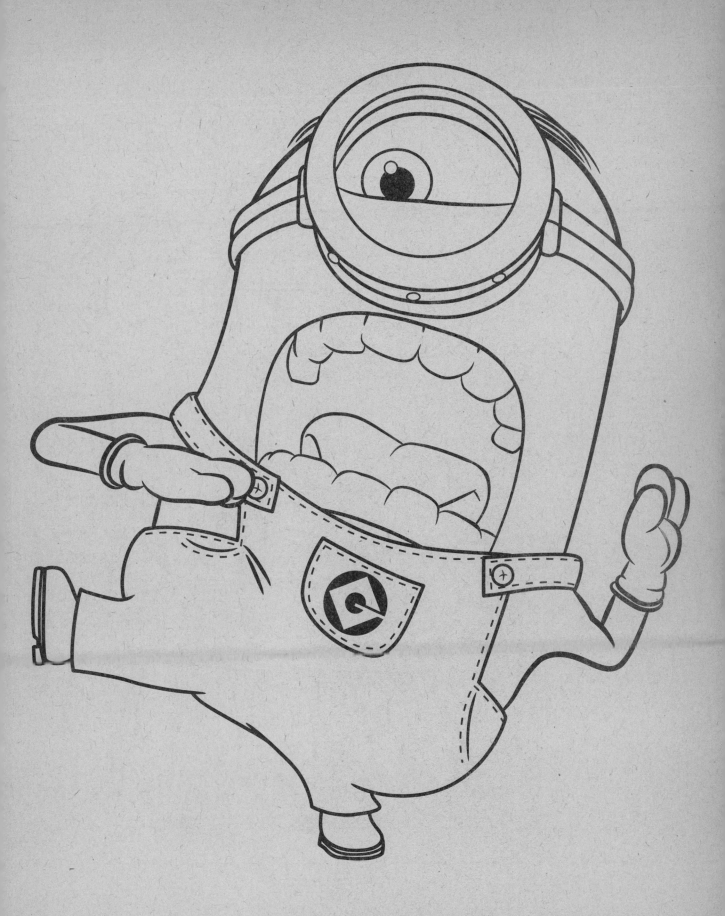

Minion Powered

Dalmatian Press

Let's hula!

Use the grid to draw Tom.

I don't share.

Which pieces complete the picture?

A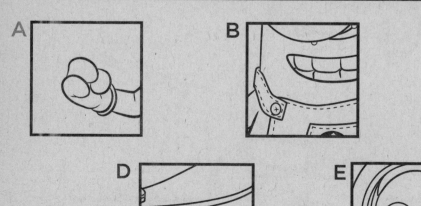

B

C

D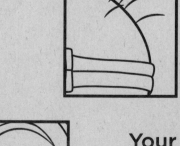

E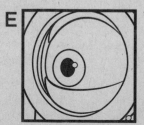

Your Answers:

☐ & ☐

Hug a Minion

Match the Minion to the correct shadow.

Testing 1-2-3.

Oops!

It's so hard to be good.

Proud to be a Minion

Uh-oh. . .

I <3 8)

Kyle is so sweet.

Think of words that start with the letters in the name Margo. Two have been done for you.

	Name	Food	Animal	Place
M				
A				
R			RHINO	
G				
O	OPAL			

Our happy despicable family.

Yellow is no longer mellow.

I <3 Gru

>:p

>:p

You say Goodbye and I say Yellow.

Gru: 1 World: 0

A Minion in shining armor.

Think of words that start with the letters in the name Antonio. Three have been done for you.

	Name	Food	Animal	Place
A				
N			Newt	
T				
O				
N				
I		Iceberg Lettuce		
O	OPAL			

Dalmatian Press

It's a Minion thing, you wouldn't understand.

Get Despicable

Which pieces complete the picture?

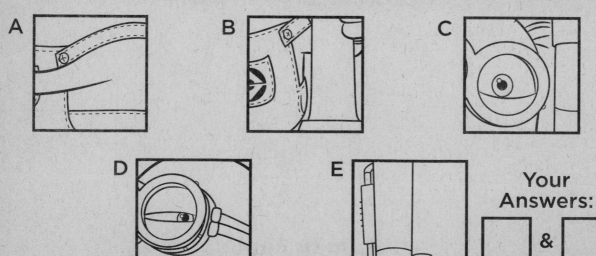

A

B

C

D

E

Family First

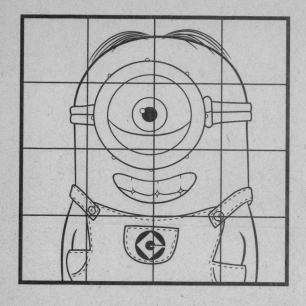

Use the grid to draw Dave.

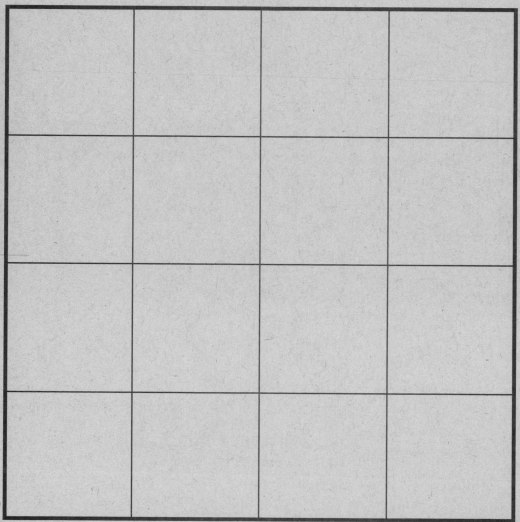

Yellow Ops

Have you hugged your Minion today?

Thanks a Minion!

You say Despicable like it's a bad thing.

It's a wild ride!

Need More Data

>:(

Kyle is a good guard dog.

Evil 101

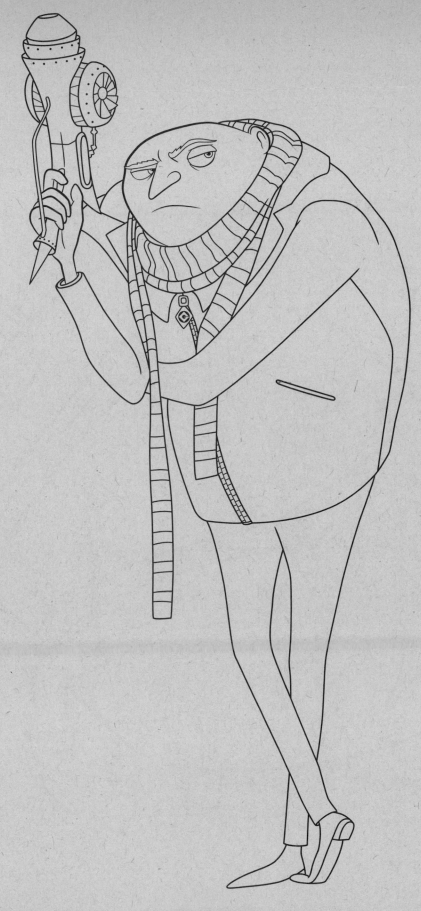

Minion and proud of it!

Best. Minion. Ever.

Medieval Minion

Mission Accomplished

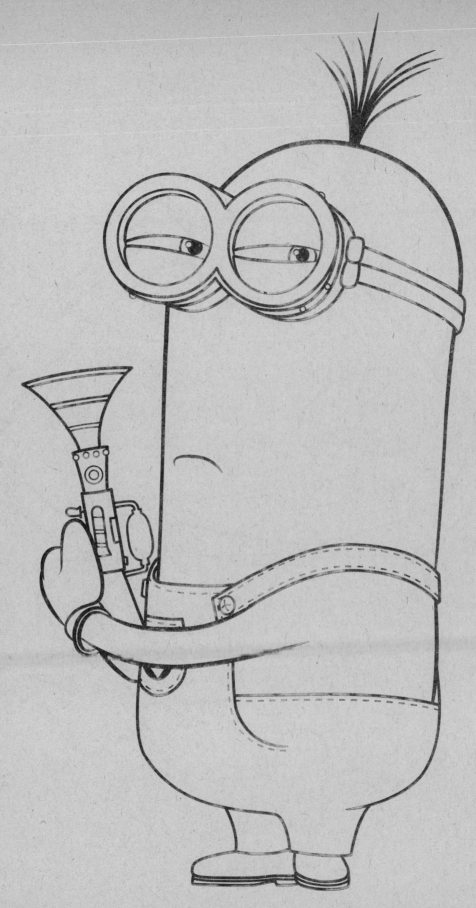

Mischievous Minion

All in favor, say "eye!"

You say Poopaye! I say Bello!

Modern Minion

Help Stuart find his way to Dave.

Eye eye, captain!

A Minion is a terrible thing to waste.

Failure is always an option.

So happy to spy you.

Yellow Bello!

Minion Power

Which Minion is different?

Eye-con

Proud to be a Minion!